I0401333

BEYOND THE REEL

The Gambling Addiction Cycle

Asa Eccleston Kibilski

Copyright © 2024 Asa Eccleston Kibilski

All rights reserved

The characters and events portrayed in this book are fictitious. Any similarity to real persons, living or dead, is coincidental and not intended by the author.

No part of this book may be reproduced, or stored in a retrieval system, or transmitted in any form or by any means, electronic, mechanical, photocopying, recording, or otherwise, without express written permission of the publisher.

CONTENTS

THE SIREN SONG: THE ALLURE AND ILLUSION OF CONTROL

The flashing lights, the clatter of chips, the rhythmic whir of the roulette wheel. These are the sights and sounds that beckon to us, promising excitement, fortune, and escape. For some, gambling is a harmless diversion, a way to unwind and test their luck. But for others, it becomes an obsession, a siren song that lures them into a dangerous cycle of risk and reward.

It all begins innocently enough. A trip to the casino with friends, a flutter on the football, a scratch card bought on a whim. The initial thrill of winning, even a small amount, triggers a rush of dopamine in our brains, the same neurotransmitter responsible for feelings of pleasure and motivation. This chemical reaction reinforces the behavior, making us crave the next win, the next high.

But the odds are rarely in our favor. Casinos and gambling machines are meticulously designed to keep us playing, to maximize the house's profits. Slot machines, for example, use sophisticated algorithms to create the illusion of near misses, those tantalizing moments when the symbols almost align, just out of reach. These near misses trigger a powerful emotional response, leading us to believe that the next spin will be the lucky one.

Similarly, roulette wheels are carefully balanced to ensure a consistent house edge, while card games like blackjack and poker involve elements of skill, they are ultimately games of chance. Even the most skilled players can experience losing streaks, and the house always has a statistical advantage.

The allure of gambling lies not just in the prospect of winning, but also in the illusion of control. We believe that we can outsmart the system, that we can develop strategies to beat the odds. This belief is reinforced by the occasional win, which fuels our confidence and keeps us coming back for more.

But the truth is, gambling addiction is not about skill or control. It's about a complex interplay of biological, psychological, and social factors. Our brains are wired to seek rewards, and gambling provides a powerful and immediate source of gratification. The thrill of winning, the anticipation of the next bet, the social aspect of gambling – these are all factors that contribute to the addictive cycle.

For those who fall into the trap of gambling addiction, the consequences can be devastating. Financial ruin, broken relationships, job loss, and even suicide are all too common outcomes. The cycle of chasing losses and trying to regain control can lead to a downward spiral of despair and desperation.

But there is hope. With the right support and treatment, it is possible to break free from the grip of gambling addiction. By understanding the underlying causes of the addiction, developing coping mechanisms, and seeking professional help, individuals can reclaim their lives and find new sources of fulfillment.

In the following chapters, we will explore the science behind gambling addiction, the psychological and neurological mechanisms that drive it, and the strategies for recovery. We will hear from individuals who have struggled with gambling addiction and learn about their journeys to healing. We will also examine the social and economic impact of gambling and discuss ways to prevent and treat this often hidden problem.

Whether you are a gambler yourself, a loved one of someone struggling with addiction, or simply interested in learning more about this complex issue, this book is for you. By understanding the allure and illusion of control that gambling offers, we can take the first steps towards a life beyond the reel.

CHASING THE DRAGON: UNDERSTANDING THE DOPAMINE RUSH

The thrill of victory, the agony of defeat – these are the emotional extremes that gamblers experience. But what is it about gambling that creates such a powerful emotional response? The answer lies in the brain's reward system, specifically the neurotransmitter dopamine.

Dopamine is a chemical messenger that plays a crucial role in motivation, pleasure, and reinforcement learning. When we experience something pleasurable, dopamine is released in the brain, creating a feeling of euphoria and a desire to repeat the behavior. This is why we enjoy activities like eating, sex, and social interaction – they trigger dopamine release and make us feel good.

Gambling, too, activates the brain's reward system, triggering a surge of dopamine that can be even more intense than that produced by natural rewards. The anticipation of winning, the thrill of risk-taking, and the excitement of the game all contribute to this dopamine rush.

But there's a catch. The dopamine rush associated with gambling is not sustained. It's a fleeting high that quickly fades, leaving the gambler craving more. This is why gamblers often chase losses, hoping to recapture the initial thrill of winning.

The problem is that the brain adapts to the dopamine rush over time. The more we gamble, the less dopamine our brains produce in response to the same level of stimulation. This means that we need to gamble more frequently and with higher stakes to achieve the same level of excitement and reward.

This phenomenon is known as tolerance, and it's a hallmark of addiction. Just like a drug addict needs to increase their dosage to get the same high, a gambling addict needs to gamble more to feel the same thrill.

But the brain's reward system is not the only factor at play in gambling addiction. Other neurotransmitters, such as serotonin and norepinephrine, also contribute to the emotional and behavioral changes associated with addiction.

Serotonin is a neurotransmitter that regulates mood, appetite, and sleep. Low levels of serotonin have been linked to depression, anxiety, and impulsivity – all of which can increase the risk of gambling addiction.

Norepinephrine is a neurotransmitter that plays a role in alertness, arousal, and stress response. High levels of norepinephrine can lead to hyperarousal and increased risk-taking behavior, which can also contribute to gambling addiction.

The complex interplay of these neurotransmitters creates a perfect storm for addiction. The dopamine rush provides the initial reward, while the changes in serotonin and norepinephrine contribute to the emotional and behavioral changes that make it difficult to quit.

It's important to note that not everyone who gambles becomes addicted. Just like some people are more susceptible to drug addiction than others, some people are more vulnerable to gambling addiction due to genetic, environmental, and psychological factors.

If you or someone you know is struggling with gambling addiction, it's important to seek professional help. There are a variety of treatment options available, including therapy, medication, and support groups. With the right support, it is possible to overcome gambling addiction and reclaim your life.

THE HOUSE ALWAYS WINS: DECODING THE MATH BEHIND THE GAMES

The allure of gambling often stems from the belief that we can beat the odds, that with the right strategy or a lucky streak, we can walk away a winner. However, the truth is more sobering: the house always has a built-in advantage, mathematically designed to ensure its profitability in the long run. Understanding this mathematical reality is crucial in dispelling the illusion of control and making informed decisions about gambling.

The House Edge: The Unshakable Advantage

At the heart of every casino game is the house edge, a percentage that represents the average profit the casino expects to make from each bet placed. This edge varies from game to game, but it's always there, working tirelessly in the casino's favor.

- **Slot Machines:** These are notorious for having high house edges, often ranging from 5% to 15%. This means that for every £100 wagered, the casino expects to keep £5 to £15, on average. The outcomes of slot machines are determined by random number generators (RNGs), ensuring that each spin is independent of the previous one and that no strategy can consistently overcome the house edge.
- **Roulette:** The house edge in roulette depends on the type of wheel. American roulette, with its double zero (00) slot, has a higher house edge of 5.26%, while European roulette, with a single zero (0), has a lower edge of 2.7%. This seemingly small difference can significantly impact your chances of winning over time.
- **Blackjack:** Considered one of the most favorable casino games for players, blackjack has a house edge that can be as

low as 0.5% when played with optimal strategy. However, most players don't use perfect strategy, and the house edge can easily creep up to 2% or more.

- **Poker:** In poker, the house doesn't directly compete against the players. Instead, it takes a rake, a percentage of each pot, as its fee for hosting the game. While skilled players can consistently win in poker, it's important to remember that the rake is always there, chipping away at their profits.

Probability vs. Payouts: The Misleading Balance

One of the most common misconceptions about gambling is that the payouts reflect the true probability of winning. However, the payouts are always slightly lower than the actual odds, ensuring that the house edge remains intact.

For example, in American roulette, there are 38 possible outcomes (1-36, 0, and 00). Betting on a single number pays out 35:1, but the true odds of winning are 37:1. This discrepancy is the house edge in action, ensuring that the casino makes a profit over time.

The Gambler's Fallacy: The Illusion of Patterns

Another common pitfall for gamblers is the gambler's fallacy, the belief that past events can influence future outcomes in games of chance. For example, after a series of red outcomes in roulette, a player might believe that black is "due" to come up next. However, each spin of the wheel is independent of the previous ones, and the probability of red or black remains the same for each spin.

The Bottom Line: Accept the Odds, Gamble Responsibly

Understanding the math behind casino games is not about discouraging gambling altogether. It's about empowering yourself with knowledge so that you can make informed decisions. By accepting the house edge and the inherent unpredictability of games of chance, you can approach gambling with realistic expectations and avoid falling into the trap of chasing losses or believing in false patterns.

Remember, gambling should be a form of entertainment, not a way to make money. Set a budget, stick to it, and never gamble more than you can afford to lose. And if you find yourself struggling to control your gambling, don't hesitate to seek help. There are resources available to support you on your journey to recovery.

FROM FUN TO FIXATION: HOW GAMBLING HABITS FORM

The journey from casual gambling to a full-blown addiction is rarely a sudden leap. Instead, it's a gradual process, a subtle shift in behavior and mindset that can easily go unnoticed until it's too late. Understanding how gambling habits form is crucial in recognizing the early warning signs and taking steps to prevent the escalation into addiction.

The Initial Hook: The Lure of Novelty and Excitement

For most people, gambling begins as a form of entertainment. The thrill of risk-taking, the social atmosphere of casinos, the anticipation of winning – these are all factors that draw people to gambling. The initial experience can be exhilarating, a welcome escape from the stresses of daily life.

The brain plays a significant role in this initial attraction. As we discussed in Chapter 2, gambling triggers the release of dopamine, the "feel-good" neurotransmitter that reinforces pleasurable experiences. This dopamine rush creates a positive association with gambling, making us want to repeat the behavior.

The Power of Intermittent Reinforcement: The "Maybe Next Time" Mentality

The problem is that gambling is based on intermittent reinforcement. This means that wins are unpredictable and infrequent, interspersed with losses. This unpredictability creates a powerful psychological effect, as it keeps us constantly hoping for the next win.

Think of it like a slot machine: most of the time, you'll lose, but the occasional win keeps you pulling the lever, hoping that the next spin will be the lucky one. This "maybe next time" mentality is a key factor in the development of gambling habits.

The Role of Cognitive Distortions: Seeing What We Want to See

Our brains are not always objective when it comes to gambling. We tend to remember our wins more vividly than our losses, a phenomenon known as selective memory. We also overestimate our skills and underestimate the role of chance, a cognitive distortion known as the illusion of control.

These cognitive distortions can lead us to believe that we're better at gambling than we actually are, and that we can control the outcome of the game. This false sense of confidence can fuel our desire to keep gambling, even when we're losing.

The Escalation: Chasing Losses and Increasing Stakes

As gambling becomes more frequent, the stakes often increase. This can happen gradually, as we try to recoup our losses, or it can happen suddenly, as we seek bigger thrills and higher payouts.

The escalation of gambling behavior is often accompanied by changes in mood and behavior. We may become more irritable, anxious, or secretive. We may start neglecting our responsibilities, borrowing money, or even engaging in illegal activities to fund our gambling.

The Point of No Return: When Habit Becomes Addiction

The line between a gambling habit and a full-blown addiction can be blurred. However, there are some key indicators that suggest a problem has developed:

- **Loss of Control:** You find it difficult to stop gambling, even when you're losing money or experiencing negative consequences.
- **Preoccupation:** You spend a significant amount of time thinking about gambling, planning your next bet, or reliving past wins.
- **Chasing Losses:** You try to recoup your losses by gambling

more, often with higher stakes.

- **Withdrawal Symptoms:** You experience irritability, restlessness, or anxiety when you try to stop gambling.
- **Secrecy and Deception:** You hide your gambling from loved ones or lie about how much you're spending.

If you recognize these signs in yourself or someone you know, it's important to seek help. Gambling addiction is a serious problem, but with the right treatment and support, it can be overcome.

LOST IN THE LABYRINTH: NAVIGATING THE SIGNS OF ADDICTION

The path to gambling addiction is often a winding one, filled with twists and turns that can be difficult to navigate. Recognizing the signs of addiction, both in yourself and in others, is crucial for early intervention and successful recovery. This chapter will delve into the behavioral, emotional, and financial red flags that signal a growing problem with gambling.

Behavioral Changes: The Telltale Signs

- **Increased Preoccupation:** One of the earliest signs of a gambling problem is an increasing preoccupation with gambling. Thoughts of the next bet, reliving past wins, and constantly seeking out opportunities to gamble can dominate a person's mind. This preoccupation can lead to neglect of other interests and responsibilities.
- **Chasing Losses:** The desire to recoup losses is a common symptom of addiction. A gambler may continue to bet, often with increasing amounts of money, in an attempt to win back what they have lost. This behavior can quickly spiral out of control, leading to significant financial problems.
- **Secrecy and Deception:** As the problem worsens, individuals may start to hide their gambling from loved ones. They may lie about where they have been, how much money they have spent, or even fabricate stories to cover up their activities.
- **Changes in Mood and Personality:** Gambling addiction can cause significant changes in a person's mood and personality. They may become more irritable, anxious, or depressed. They may also experience mood swings, becoming elated after a win and despondent after a loss.

- **Neglect of Responsibilities:** As gambling takes center stage, other areas of life may begin to suffer. Work performance may decline, relationships may deteriorate, and personal hygiene may be neglected.

Emotional Distress: The Hidden Toll

- **Anxiety and Depression:** The stress and anxiety associated with gambling can lead to or exacerbate existing mental health conditions. The shame and guilt of hiding the problem can also contribute to feelings of depression.
- **Irritability and Anger:** The frustration of losing, the stress of financial problems, and the pressure to hide the addiction can lead to outbursts of anger and irritability.
- **Hopelessness and Despair:** As the problem worsens, individuals may feel trapped in a cycle of addiction they cannot escape. This can lead to feelings of hopelessness and despair, increasing the risk of self-harm or suicide.

Financial Red Flags: The Domino Effect

- **Unexplained Debt:** One of the most obvious signs of a gambling problem is unexplained debt. This can include credit card debt, loans, or even borrowing from friends and family.
- **Financial Secrecy:** An individual with a gambling problem may become secretive about their finances, hiding bank statements, bills, or other financial documents.
- **Unexplained Missing Money:** If money seems to disappear without explanation, it could be a sign that it is being spent on gambling.
- **Financial Strain:** The financial strain of gambling addiction can lead to serious consequences, such as bankruptcy, foreclosure, or even homelessness.

Recognizing the Signs: A Call to Action

If you recognize these signs in yourself or someone you love, it's important to seek help as soon as possible. Gambling addiction is a treatable condition, and early intervention can significantly improve the chances of recovery. There are many resources available, including therapy, support groups, and helplines. Remember, you are not alone, and there is hope for a brighter future.

In the next chapter, we will explore the neurological underpinnings of gambling addiction, delving into the fascinating world of the gambler's brain.

THE GAMBLER'S BRAIN: NEUROSCIENCE AND THE CYCLE OF CRAVING

Gambling addiction is not simply a matter of weak willpower or poor decision-making. It's a complex condition rooted in the intricate workings of the brain. Understanding the neurological mechanisms behind gambling addiction can help us to better comprehend the challenges faced by those struggling with this disorder and to develop more effective treatment strategies.

The Dopamine Reward Pathway: The Pleasure Circuit Hijacked

As we've discussed in previous chapters, the neurotransmitter dopamine plays a pivotal role in gambling addiction. Dopamine is the brain's "feel-good" chemical, released in response to pleasurable experiences like eating, sex, and social interaction. Gambling, too, triggers a surge of dopamine, creating a sense of euphoria and reinforcing the desire to continue gambling.

However, in the gambler's brain, the dopamine reward pathway becomes dysregulated. The brain's natural ability to regulate dopamine production is disrupted, leading to a heightened sensitivity to gambling-related stimuli. This means that even the anticipation of gambling can trigger a dopamine surge, creating a powerful craving that can be difficult to resist.

The Role of the Prefrontal Cortex: Impaired Decision-Making

The prefrontal cortex is the part of the brain responsible for executive functions, such as decision-making, impulse control, and planning. In individuals with gambling addiction, the prefrontal cortex shows signs of dysfunction. This impairment can lead to impulsive decision-making, difficulty assessing risks and rewards, and an inability to resist the urge to gamble.

The Insula: The Seat of Craving and Urges

The insula is a brain region involved in processing emotions, bodily sensations, and urges. In gambling addiction, the insula becomes hyperactive, amplifying the intensity of cravings and urges to gamble. This heightened activity in the insula can make it extremely difficult for individuals to resist the temptation to gamble, even when they are aware of the negative consequences.

The Cycle of Craving: A Vicious Circle

The neurological changes in the gambler's brain create a vicious cycle of craving and reward. The anticipation of gambling triggers a dopamine surge, leading to an intense craving. When the individual gambles, the dopamine rush temporarily satisfies the craving, reinforcing the behavior. However, the dopamine high quickly fades, and the craving returns, leading the individual to gamble again.

This cycle can become increasingly difficult to break over time, as the brain becomes more sensitive to gambling-related stimuli and less responsive to natural rewards. The individual may need to gamble more frequently and with higher stakes to achieve the same level of satisfaction, further fueling the addiction.

Breaking the Cycle: A Multifaceted Approach

Overcoming gambling addiction requires a multifaceted approach that addresses both the neurological and psychological aspects of the disorder. Treatment options may include:

- **Cognitive Behavioral Therapy (CBT):** CBT helps individuals identify and change the thoughts and behaviors that contribute to their addiction. It can teach them coping skills to manage cravings and urges, and develop healthier ways to cope with stress and emotions.
- **Medication:** Certain medications, such as naltrexone and bupropion, have shown promise in reducing the urge to gamble and improving impulse control.

- **Support Groups:** Support groups, such as Gamblers Anonymous, provide a safe and supportive environment for individuals to share their experiences, learn from others, and receive encouragement on their recovery journey.

The Importance of Early Intervention

Early intervention is crucial in the treatment of gambling addiction. The sooner the disorder is recognized and addressed, the greater the chances of successful recovery. If you or someone you know is struggling with gambling addiction, don't hesitate to seek professional help. There is hope for a brighter future, free from the grip of addiction.

THE SLOT MACHINE SPELL: PSYCHOLOGY OF NEAR MISSES AND FALSE WINS

Slot machines are the most popular form of gambling worldwide, their mesmerizing lights and sounds captivating players and often luring them into a trance-like state. But beneath the flashy exterior lies a carefully calculated design, one that exploits human psychology to maximize player engagement and profits for the house. This chapter will delve into the psychological tricks employed by slot machines, particularly the concepts of near misses and false wins, and how they contribute to the addictive nature of these games.

The Illusion of Near Misses: So Close, Yet So Far

One of the most potent psychological tools employed by slot machines is the near miss. This occurs when the reels stop just short of a winning combination, creating the illusion that the player was on the verge of victory. This near miss triggers a surge of excitement and anticipation, leading the player to believe that the next spin will be the lucky one.

Research has shown that near misses activate the same reward pathways in the brain as actual wins, releasing dopamine and creating a pleasurable sensation. This reinforces the desire to continue playing, even in the face of repeated losses. The near miss phenomenon is particularly effective in slot machines because the outcome of each spin is determined by a random number generator (RNG), making it impossible to predict or influence the results.

The Deception of False Wins: A Pyrrhic Victory

Another psychological trick employed by slot machines is the false win. This occurs when the player wins an amount of money that is less than the amount they wagered. For example, a player may bet £1 and win back 50 pence. While technically a win, this outcome is actually a net loss for the player.

False wins are designed to create the illusion of progress and mask the overall losses. The player may feel a sense of accomplishment and continue playing, believing they are on a winning streak, even though they are slowly losing money over time. This can be particularly dangerous for players who are unaware of the concept of false wins, as they may continue to gamble based on a false sense of success.

The Role of Sound and Visual Effects: Creating an Immersive Experience

The mesmerizing lights, catchy jingles, and celebratory sounds that accompany slot machine play are not merely decorative elements. They are carefully crafted to create an immersive and stimulating experience that enhances the emotional impact of wins and near misses.

Studies have shown that the sounds associated with slot machines can trigger a physiological response in players, increasing heart rate and skin conductance. These physiological changes can create a sense of excitement and anticipation, further fueling the desire to continue playing.

The Multi-Line Deception: More Lines, More Losses

Modern slot machines often feature multiple paylines, allowing players to bet on multiple combinations of symbols simultaneously. While this may seem like an advantage, it can actually lead to more losses in the long run.

With multiple paylines, players may win small amounts on some lines while losing on others. These small wins, however, are often not enough to offset the overall losses. The illusion of winning on multiple lines can mask the fact that the player is actually losing money.

Breaking the Spell: Recognizing the Tricks and Protecting Yourself

Understanding the psychological tricks employed by slot machines is the first step in breaking their spell. By recognizing the illusory nature of near misses and false wins, you can make more informed decisions about your gambling behavior.

Here are some tips for protecting yourself from the psychological manipulation of slot machines:

- **Set a budget:** Before you start playing, decide how much money you are willing to lose and stick to it.
- **Take breaks:** Don't get caught up in the excitement of the game. Take regular breaks to clear your head and assess your situation.
- **Be aware of the time:** Time can easily slip away when you're playing slot machines. Set a time limit for your gambling session and stick to it.
- **Don't chase losses:** If you're losing, don't try to win back your money by gambling more. This is a recipe for disaster.
- **Seek help if needed:** If you're struggling to control your gambling, don't hesitate to seek professional help. There are resources available to support you on your journey to recovery.

MORE THAN LUCK: SKILL VS. CHANCE IN GAMBLING

The world of gambling is often painted with a broad brush, lumping all games together under the umbrella of chance. However, a closer look reveals a more nuanced landscape, one where skill and strategy can play a significant role alongside luck. This chapter will explore the spectrum of skill and chance in various forms of gambling, helping you understand where your abilities can make a difference and where the odds are stacked against you.

Games of Pure Chance: The Roll of the Dice

Some games are entirely based on chance, with no room for skill or strategy. Examples include:

- **Slot Machines:** As discussed in Chapter 7, the outcomes of slot machines are determined by random number generators (RNGs), making each spin independent of the previous one. No amount of skill or strategy can alter the odds of winning.
- **Roulette:** While you can choose where to place your bets in roulette, the outcome of the spin is ultimately determined by chance. The ball's landing spot is unpredictable, and no system can consistently beat the house edge.
- **Lottery:** Winning the lottery is purely a matter of luck. The numbers drawn are random, and there is no way to increase your chances of winning other than buying more tickets.

Games of Mixed Skill and Chance: Where Strategy Matters

Other games involve a combination of skill and chance, where strategic decisions can significantly impact your chances of winning. Examples include:

- **Blackjack:** Blackjack is a card game where players compete against the dealer, aiming to get a hand value as close to 21 as possible without going over. While the cards dealt are random, skilled players can use strategies like card counting and basic strategy to reduce the house edge and increase their chances of winning.

- **Poker:** Poker is a game of skill, psychology, and a bit of luck. While the cards dealt are random, skilled players can use their knowledge of probabilities, betting patterns, and opponent behavior to make informed decisions and outsmart their opponents.
- **Sports Betting:** While luck plays a role in the outcome of sporting events, skilled bettors can analyze statistics, team performance, and other factors to make informed predictions and increase their chances of winning.

The Importance of Skill: Separating Winners from Losers

In games of mixed skill and chance, the ability to make informed decisions and execute effective strategies can be the difference between winning and losing. Skilled players can consistently outperform less skilled players over time, even when luck is a factor.

However, it's important to remember that skill alone cannot guarantee a win. Even the most skilled players can experience losing streaks due to the inherent randomness of these games. The key is to focus on making sound decisions based on the information available and to avoid chasing losses or making impulsive bets.

The Illusion of Skill: The Danger of Overconfidence

In some cases, players may overestimate their skills and believe they have more control over the outcome of a game than they actually do. This illusion of skill can be particularly dangerous in games of chance, as it can lead to excessive risk-taking and overconfidence in one's ability to win.

It's important to be honest with yourself about your skill level and to recognize the role of chance in any gambling game. This will help you make more realistic decisions and avoid falling into the trap of overconfidence.

The Bottom Line: Know Your Game, Play Responsibly

Understanding the role of skill and chance in gambling is essential for making informed decisions and playing responsibly. By recognizing where your skills can be applied and where luck plays a dominant role, you can approach gambling with realistic expectations and avoid falling into the trap of chasing losses or believing in false patterns.

Remember, gambling should be a form of entertainment, not a way to make money. Set a budget, stick to it, and never gamble more than you can afford to lose. And if you find yourself struggling to control your gambling, don't hesitate to seek help. There are resources available to support you on your journey to recovery.

WHEN THE WHEELS STOP SPINNING: FINANCIAL RUIN AND DEBT SPIRALS

The allure of gambling often hinges on the dream of striking it rich, of turning a small wager into a life-changing fortune. But for many, this dream turns into a nightmare, as the pursuit of riches leads to financial ruin and a downward spiral of debt. This chapter will explore the devastating financial consequences of gambling addiction, the psychological factors that contribute to financial mismanagement, and strategies for regaining control of your finances.

The Slippery Slope: From Small Bets to Big Losses

Gambling addiction rarely starts with a catastrophic loss. It often begins with small bets, seemingly harmless amounts of money that gradually escalate as the gambler chases losses or seeks bigger thrills. The intermittent reinforcement of wins, as discussed in Chapter 4, can create a false sense of control and lead to increasingly risky behavior.

The gambler's brain, as we explored in Chapter 6, is wired to seek rewards, and the dopamine rush associated with gambling can override rational decision-making. This can lead to impulsive betting, chasing losses, and ignoring financial limits.

The Cost of Chasing Losses: A Vicious Cycle

One of the most dangerous aspects of gambling addiction is the tendency to chase losses. When a gambler loses money, they may feel compelled to gamble more in an attempt to recoup their losses. This can lead to a vicious cycle, where the gambler keeps losing and betting more, digging themselves deeper into a financial hole.

The psychological pressure to chase losses can be immense. Gamblers may feel ashamed or guilty about their losses, and they may believe that they can win back their money if they just keep playing. This irrational thinking can lead to reckless behavior and devastating financial consequences.

The Debt Trap: Borrowing to Fuel the Addiction

As gambling losses mount, individuals may turn to borrowing money to fuel their addiction. This can include credit cards, loans, or even borrowing from friends and family. The debt can quickly spiral out of control, as the gambler struggles to make payments and continues to gamble in an attempt to win back enough money to cover their debts.

The stress and anxiety of debt can exacerbate the gambling problem, creating a vicious cycle where the gambler feels trapped and desperate. The shame and guilt of accumulating debt can also lead to further emotional distress and isolation.

Financial Ruin: The Devastating Consequences

The financial consequences of gambling addiction can be catastrophic. Individuals may lose their savings, their homes, their cars, and even their jobs. The financial strain can lead to bankruptcy, homelessness, and other devastating outcomes.

The impact of financial ruin extends beyond the individual gambler. It can also affect their families, friends, and communities. Spouses and partners may be forced to bear the financial burden, relationships may be strained, and children may suffer from neglect or emotional trauma.

Regaining Control: Strategies for Financial Recovery

Recovering from the financial devastation of gambling addiction is a long and difficult process. It requires a commitment to change, professional help, and the support of loved ones.

Here are some strategies for regaining control of your finances:

- **Seek professional help:** Financial advisors and credit counselors can help you develop a plan to manage your debt and rebuild your financial life.
- **Create a budget:** A budget can help you track your income and expenses, identify areas where you can cut back, and prioritize debt repayment.
- **Stop gambling:** This may seem obvious, but it's the most important step in financial recovery. Seek help from a therapist or support group to address the underlying addiction.
- **Be transparent with loved ones:** Share your financial situation with your loved ones and ask for their support. They can offer emotional support and help you stay accountable to your financial goals.
- **Be patient:** Financial recovery takes time and effort. Don't get discouraged by setbacks, and celebrate your successes along the way.

Remember, you are not alone in this journey. Many people have overcome gambling addiction and rebuilt their financial lives. With the right support and resources, you can too.

HIDDEN PAIN: IMPACT ON RELATIONSHIPS AND MENTAL HEALTH

While the financial consequences of gambling addiction are often the most visible, the emotional and relational toll can be equally devastating, leaving deep scars that can take years to heal. This chapter will delve into the hidden pain of gambling addiction, exploring its impact on relationships, mental health, and overall well-being.

The Erosion of Trust: A House of Cards

At the heart of any healthy relationship lies trust. Gambling addiction, with its web of secrecy and deception, can erode this foundation, leaving relationships fragile and vulnerable.

- **Lies and Betrayal:** As the addiction progresses, individuals may resort to lying and manipulation to conceal their gambling activities. They may hide financial statements, fabricate stories about their whereabouts, or even steal money from loved ones. These acts of betrayal can shatter trust and create deep rifts in relationships.
- **Broken Promises:** Gamblers often make promises to quit or cut back, only to break them repeatedly. This cycle of broken promises can lead to feelings of resentment, anger, and disappointment in loved ones.
- **Emotional Distance:** As the gambler becomes more preoccupied with gambling, they may withdraw emotionally from their loved ones. They may become less affectionate, less communicative, and less interested in participating in family activities. This emotional distance can leave loved ones feeling neglected, hurt, and alone.

The Crushing Weight of Shame and Guilt: A Heavy Burden

Gambling addiction is often accompanied by intense feelings of shame and guilt. Individuals may feel ashamed of their behavior, guilty for the pain they have caused their loved ones, and worthless for their inability to control their addiction.

- **Social Isolation:** Shame and guilt can lead to social isolation, as individuals withdraw from social activities and avoid contact with friends and family. This isolation can further exacerbate feelings of loneliness and depression.
- **Self-Loathing:** The internalized shame and guilt associated with gambling addiction can lead to self-loathing and a negative self-image. Individuals may believe they are irredeemable and undeserving of love and support.

Mental Health Crisis: The Dark Side of Addiction

Gambling addiction is strongly linked to mental health problems, including:

- **Depression:** The financial stress, relationship problems, and feelings of shame and guilt associated with gambling addiction can trigger or worsen depression.
- **Anxiety:** The constant worry about money, the fear of being caught, and the pressure to gamble can lead to high levels of anxiety.
- **Substance Abuse:** Individuals with gambling addiction may turn to alcohol or drugs to cope with their emotional distress or to numb the pain of their losses.
- **Suicidal Thoughts:** In severe cases, the despair and hopelessness of gambling addiction can lead to suicidal thoughts and behaviors.

The Ripple Effect: Impact on Loved Ones

The impact of gambling addiction extends far beyond the individual. Family members and friends often suffer silently, bearing the brunt of the emotional and financial fallout.

- **Children:** Children of gambling addicts may experience neglect, emotional instability, and financial hardship. They may also be at increased risk of developing gambling problems themselves.
- **Spouses and Partners:** Spouses and partners of gambling addicts may experience financial strain, emotional distress, and a loss of trust in the relationship.
- **Friends:** Friends may feel helpless and frustrated as they watch their loved one spiral out of control. They may also feel betrayed by the lies and deception associated with the addiction.

Healing the Wounds: A Path to Recovery

While the emotional and relational damage caused by gambling addiction can be profound, it is not irreversible. Recovery is possible, but it requires a commitment to change, professional help, and the support of loved ones.

Therapy can help individuals address the underlying emotional issues that contribute to their addiction, such as depression, anxiety, or trauma. It can also teach them coping skills to manage stress and resist the urge to gamble.

Support groups, such as Gamblers Anonymous, provide a safe and supportive environment for individuals to share their experiences, learn from others, and receive encouragement on their recovery journey.

Family therapy can help repair damaged relationships and rebuild trust. It can also teach family members how to support their loved one's recovery and how to cope with the emotional impact of the addiction.

Recovery may be long and challenging, but it is possible to heal the wounds of gambling addiction and rebuild a life filled with healthy relationships, emotional well-being, and financial stability.

THROUGH A LOVED ONE'S EYES: UNDERSTANDING THE FAMILY'S BURDEN

Gambling addiction is not an individual struggle; it casts a long shadow over the lives of loved ones, leaving them grappling with emotional turmoil, financial instability, and a profound sense of betrayal. This chapter aims to provide insight into the experiences of family members and friends affected by gambling addiction, offering a glimpse into their pain, confusion, and the arduous journey towards healing.

The Initial Denial: A Refusal to See

In the early stages of gambling addiction, loved ones may be oblivious to the growing problem. The gambler may skillfully conceal their activities, masking their losses and downplaying the time spent gambling. Family members may notice subtle changes in behavior – increased irritability, financial strain, or a growing obsession with sports or games of chance – but they may dismiss these as temporary stressors or harmless hobbies.

The Crumbling Facade: Cracks in the Foundation

As the addiction progresses, the cracks in the facade become harder to ignore. Unexplained absences, secretive phone calls, and mounting debt raise alarm bells. Loved ones may confront the gambler, only to be met with denial, anger, or promises to change that are quickly broken. The gambler may become skilled at manipulating their loved ones, using guilt, charm, or emotional blackmail to maintain their secrecy and continue their destructive behavior.

The Rollercoaster of Emotions: From Hope to Despair

Living with a gambling addict is an emotional rollercoaster. Loved ones may experience a wide range of emotions, often cycling through them in a matter of days or even hours.

- **Hope:** Each time the gambler promises to quit or seeks help, loved ones may feel a surge of hope, believing that this time will be different.
- **Disappointment:** When the gambler relapses or breaks their promises, loved ones may feel deep disappointment and a sense of betrayal.
- **Anger:** The lies, manipulation, and financial strain can lead to anger and resentment towards the gambler.
- **Guilt:** Loved ones may blame themselves for the addiction, wondering if they could have done something differently to prevent it.
- **Fear:** The uncertainty of the future, the fear of financial ruin, and the worry about the gambler's well-being can create a constant state of anxiety.

The Financial Fallout: A Shared Burden

The financial consequences of gambling addiction are not borne solely by the gambler. Family members often find themselves sharing the burden, struggling to make ends meet, paying off debts, and facing the threat of financial ruin.

- **Loss of Savings:** The gambler may drain family savings, retirement funds, or college funds to fuel their addiction.
- **Debt Accumulation:** Loved ones may be forced to take on debt to cover the gambler's losses or to pay for basic necessities.
- **Financial Instability:** The constant drain on finances can create a sense of instability and insecurity, making it difficult to plan for the future.
- **Strained Relationships:** Financial stress can strain relationships, leading to arguments, resentment, and even divorce.

The Toll on Mental Health: A Silent Suffering

The emotional and financial strain of living with a gambling addict can take a significant toll on the mental health of loved ones.

- **Depression:** The constant worry, disappointment, and sense of betrayal can lead to depression and feelings of hopelessness.
- **Anxiety:** The uncertainty of the future and the fear of financial ruin can trigger anxiety and panic attacks.
- **Stress-Related Illnesses:** The chronic stress of living with a gambling addict can manifest in physical symptoms, such as headaches, insomnia, and digestive problems.
- **Codependency:** Loved ones may develop codependent behaviors, enabling the gambler's addiction by covering up their actions, making excuses for them, or rescuing them from financial crises.

Remember, you are not alone in this journey. Millions of families are affected by gambling addiction, and there are resources available to help you navigate this difficult path. By seeking support and prioritizing your own well-being, you can reclaim your life and find hope for a brighter future.

HITTING ROCK BOTTOM: THE MOMENT OF TRUTH

The descent into gambling addiction is often a gradual process, a slow erosion of self-control and financial stability that can be difficult to recognize until it's too late. However, for many, there comes a pivotal moment, a stark realization that their life has spiraled out of control. This is the moment of hitting rock bottom, a turning point that can either lead to despair and self-destruction or ignite the spark of recovery.

The Crumbling Edifice: When the Walls Come Crashing Down

Rock bottom can manifest in different ways for different people. It could be a financial catastrophe, such as losing a home, declaring bankruptcy, or facing legal charges for theft or fraud. It could be a relational crisis, such as a spouse leaving, losing custody of children, or being ostracized by friends and family. It could also be a personal crisis, such as a suicide attempt, a mental breakdown, or a health scare triggered by the stress and strain of addiction.

Regardless of its specific form, rock bottom is a moment of reckoning, a shattering of the illusion that the gambler can control their addiction or escape its consequences. The walls they have built around themselves, the lies they have told, and the denial they have clung to, all come crashing down.

The Emotional Maelstrom: A Whirlwind of Pain

Hitting rock bottom is a profoundly painful experience. It's a moment of deep despair, shame, and self-loathing. The gambler may feel like a failure, a burden to their loved ones, and a complete and utter disappointment to themselves.

The emotional turmoil can be overwhelming, leading to a range of intense emotions, including:

- **Shame:** The realization of the harm they have caused to themselves and others can trigger intense feelings of shame.
- **Guilt:** The gambler may feel guilty for the pain they have inflicted on their loved ones, the financial losses they have caused, and the trust they have broken.
- **Anger:** They may feel angry at themselves for their weakness, at the gambling industry for its predatory practices, or at the world for its perceived unfairness.
- **Depression:** The loss of hope, the feeling of being trapped, and the weight of guilt and shame can lead to a deep depression.
- **Despair:** The gambler may feel like there is no way out, that their life is ruined, and that they are doomed to a life of misery and addiction.

The Turning Point: A Choice to Be Made

While hitting rock bottom is a devastating experience, it can also be a catalyst for change. The pain and despair can become so overwhelming that the gambler is finally ready to admit their powerlessness over the addiction and seek help.

The moment of truth presents a choice:

- **Continue the downward spiral:** The gambler can choose to continue on the destructive path of addiction, numbing the pain with more gambling, substance abuse, or other self-destructive behaviors. This path leads to further isolation, despair, and potentially even death.
- **Embrace recovery:** The gambler can choose to turn their life around, to seek help, and to embark on a journey of recovery. This path requires courage, humility, and a willingness to face the pain and consequences of their actions. But it also offers the promise of hope, healing, and a new beginning.

The Road to Redemption: A Journey of Healing

The road to recovery from gambling addiction is not easy. It requires a commitment to change, professional help, and the support of loved ones. But for those who are willing to take the first step, there is hope for a brighter future.

Recovery involves addressing the underlying causes of the addiction, developing coping mechanisms to manage cravings and triggers, and rebuilding a life based on healthy values and goals. It also involves repairing damaged relationships, making amends for past mistakes, and finding new sources of meaning and purpose.

The journey may be long and challenging, but it is possible to overcome gambling addiction and create a life of freedom, fulfillment, and joy.

BREAKING FREE: THE FIRST STEPS TO RECOVERY

Hitting rock bottom can be a wake-up call, a moment of clarity that ignites the desire for change. However, the path to recovery from gambling addiction is not always straightforward. It requires courage, perseverance, and a willingness to confront the underlying issues that fueled the addiction. This chapter will explore the initial steps towards breaking free from the grip of gambling, offering guidance and support for those who are ready to embark on this transformative journey.

Acknowledging the Problem: The First Hurdle

The first step to recovery is acknowledging that there is a problem. This may seem obvious, but for many, admitting to a gambling addiction is a difficult and humbling experience. Denial, shame, and fear can prevent individuals from seeking help, keeping them trapped in a cycle of self-destruction.

Recognizing the signs of addiction, as discussed in Chapter 5, is crucial in this process. If you find yourself exhibiting these signs or if loved ones have expressed concern about your gambling behavior, it's important to take their concerns seriously.

Once you have acknowledged the problem, the next step is to reach out for help. This can be a daunting prospect, but it's essential for successful recovery. There are many resources available to help you on your journey, including:

- **Therapists and Counselors:** Trained professionals can provide guidance and support, helping you understand the root causes of your addiction and develop coping mechanisms to manage cravings and triggers.
- **Support Groups:** Gamblers Anonymous (GA) and other support groups offer a safe and supportive environment

where you can connect with others who are going through similar experiences. Sharing your story and hearing from others can be incredibly empowering and motivating.

- **Helplines:** National and local helplines can provide confidential support and information about treatment options.
- **Family and Friends:** Talking to trusted loved ones can be a crucial step in breaking free from addiction. Their support and encouragement can be invaluable on your journey to recovery.

Taking Action: Steps Towards Change

Recovery is not a passive process; it requires active participation and a willingness to make changes. Here are some initial steps you can take to start your journey towards recovery:

- **Stop Gambling:** This may seem obvious, but it's the most important step. If you're struggling to stop on your own, seek help from a professional or support group.
- **Identify Triggers:** Recognize the situations, emotions, or people that trigger your urge to gamble. Avoiding these triggers can help you stay on track.
- **Develop Coping Mechanisms:** Learn healthy ways to cope with stress, anxiety, boredom, and other emotions that may trigger gambling. This could include exercise, meditation, hobbies, or spending time with loved ones.
- **Manage Your Finances:** Take control of your finances by creating a budget, paying off debts, and avoiding situations where you might be tempted to gamble.
- **Build a Support Network:** Surround yourself with supportive people who understand your struggles and encourage your recovery.

The Road Ahead: A Journey of Self-Discovery

Recovery from gambling addiction is not a quick fix; it's a lifelong journey of self-discovery and growth. There will be challenges and setbacks along the way, but with perseverance and the right support, you can overcome this addiction and build a fulfilling life free from the grip of gambling.

Every step you take towards healing is a victory, and every day you choose not to gamble is a testament to your strength and resilience.

SEEKING HELP: FINDING SUPPORT AND COMMUNITY

The journey to recovery from gambling addiction is not one to be taken alone. While the decision to change must come from within, seeking external support is crucial for navigating the complexities of addiction and building a sustainable path to healing. This chapter will explore the various forms of help available for individuals and their loved ones, emphasizing the power of community and connection in overcoming this challenging disorder.

Professional Help: The Cornerstone of Recovery

Professional help forms the cornerstone of recovery from gambling addiction. Therapists, counselors, and addiction specialists can provide invaluable guidance, support, and evidence-based treatments that address the root causes of addiction and help individuals develop the skills necessary for lasting change.

- **Cognitive Behavioral Therapy (CBT):** CBT is a widely used and effective form of therapy for gambling addiction. It focuses on identifying and changing the negative thoughts and behaviors that contribute to gambling, as well as developing healthy coping mechanisms to manage cravings and triggers.
- **Motivational Interviewing (MI):** MI is a collaborative approach that helps individuals explore their ambivalence about change and build motivation for recovery.
- **Medication:** In some cases, medication may be prescribed to help manage co-occurring mental health conditions, such as depression or anxiety, or to reduce the urge to gamble.
- **Financial Counseling:** Financial counselors can

help individuals struggling with gambling-related debt to develop a plan for managing their finances and rebuilding their financial stability.

Support Groups: The Power of Shared Experience

Support groups, such as Gamblers Anonymous (GA), offer a unique form of support for individuals in recovery. These groups provide a safe and non-judgmental space where individuals can share their experiences, learn from others, and receive encouragement and support on their journey to recovery.

The power of support groups lies in the shared experience of addiction. Members understand the struggles and challenges faced by others in recovery, and they can offer empathy, compassion, and practical advice based on their own experiences. The sense of community and belonging that support groups provide can be invaluable in maintaining motivation and preventing relapse.

Online Resources: Accessible Support at Your Fingertips

In today's digital age, online resources offer a wealth of information and support for individuals and families affected by gambling addiction. Online forums, chat rooms, and support groups provide a platform for connecting with others, sharing experiences, and accessing information about treatment options.

Online resources also offer a sense of anonymity, which can be helpful for those who are hesitant to seek help in person. The accessibility and convenience of online resources make them a valuable tool for individuals who may not have access to traditional support groups or therapy.

Family and Friends: A Vital Support Network

The support of family and friends is essential for recovery from gambling addiction. Loved ones can provide emotional support, encouragement, and practical assistance, such as helping to manage finances or accompanying the individual to therapy or support group meetings.

Family members can also benefit from seeking support for themselves. Groups such as Gam-Anon provide a space for loved ones to share their experiences, learn coping skills, and receive support from others who understand the unique challenges of living with a gambling addict.

Building a Community of Support: A Holistic Approach

Recovery from gambling addiction is not just about addressing the individual's behavior; it's about creating a supportive environment that fosters healing and growth. This involves building a community of support that includes professional help, support groups, online resources, and the love and support of family and friends.

By reaching out for help and connecting with others, individuals in recovery can gain the strength, encouragement, and resources they need to overcome their addiction and build a fulfilling life free from the grip of gambling. Remember, seeking help is not a sign of weakness; it's a courageous step towards a brighter future.

RETRAINING THE MIND: COGNITIVE BEHAVIORAL APPROACHES

The journey to recovery from gambling addiction is not just about stopping the behavior; it's about rewiring the brain and retraining the mind to think and act differently. Cognitive Behavioral Therapy (CBT) is a powerful tool in this process, helping individuals to identify and change the harmful thought patterns and behaviors that fuel their addiction. This chapter will explore the principles of CBT and how it can be applied to break the cycle of gambling addiction.

Understanding Cognitive Behavioral Therapy: A Mind-Body Approach

CBT is based on the idea that our thoughts, feelings, and behaviors are interconnected. Negative thoughts can lead to negative emotions, which in turn can lead to harmful behaviors. In the case of gambling addiction, these negative thoughts might include:

- **Overestimating the Odds:** Believing that you have a better chance of winning than you actually do.
- **Chasing Losses:** Believing that you can win back your losses if you just keep gambling.
- **The Illusion of Control:** Believing that you can control the outcome of the game through skill or strategy.
- **Superstitions:** Believing that certain rituals or lucky charms will increase your chances of winning.

CBT aims to challenge these negative thoughts and replace them with more realistic and helpful ones. It also teaches individuals how to cope with cravings and urges, develop healthier habits, and build a more positive self-image.

The CBT Process: A Step-by-Step Guide

1. **Identifying Negative Thoughts:** The first step in CBT is to identify the negative thoughts that trigger or exacerbate gambling behavior. This is often done through journaling, self-reflection, or talking to a therapist.

2. **Challenging Negative Thoughts:** Once negative thoughts are identified, they can be challenged with evidence and logic. For example, if a gambler believes they can win back their losses, a therapist might ask them to consider the statistical probability of this happening.

3. **Developing Coping Skills:** CBT teaches individuals healthy coping skills to manage cravings and urges to gamble. These skills might include relaxation techniques, mindfulness exercises, or distraction techniques.

4. **Changing Behaviors:** CBT also focuses on changing the behaviors that contribute to gambling addiction. This might involve avoiding triggers, setting limits on gambling, or developing new hobbies and interests.

5. **Building a Support Network:** Having a strong support network of friends, family, and therapists can be crucial for successful recovery. CBT can help individuals build and maintain these relationships.

The Power of CBT: A Proven Approach

CBT has been shown to be effective in treating a wide range of mental health disorders, including gambling addiction. Research has demonstrated that CBT can help individuals reduce their gambling behavior, improve their impulse control, and develop healthier coping mechanisms.

CBT is not a quick fix, however. It requires a commitment to change and active participation in the therapeutic process. But for those who are willing to put in the work, CBT can be a powerful tool for breaking free from the grip of gambling addiction.

Additional CBT Techniques: Expanding Your Toolkit

In addition to the core principles of CBT, there are a variety of other techniques that can be helpful in treating gambling addiction:

- **Exposure Therapy:** Gradual exposure to gambling-related stimuli in a controlled environment can help individuals reduce their reactivity and cravings over time.
- **Relapse Prevention:** Developing a plan for managing potential triggers and setbacks can help individuals stay on track in their recovery.
- **Mindfulness:** Practicing mindfulness can help individuals become more aware of their thoughts and feelings, and make more conscious choices about their behavior.
- **Self-Compassion:** Learning to be kind and understanding towards oneself can be crucial in overcoming the shame and guilt associated with addiction.

Retraining the mind is not a one-time event; it's a lifelong process. But with the right tools and support, individuals in recovery can learn to manage their thoughts and behaviors, build healthier habits, and create a fulfilling life free from the grip of gambling addiction.

HEALING THE WOUNDS: ADDRESSING UNDERLYING EMOTIONAL ISSUES

Gambling addiction rarely exists in isolation. It often coexists with or is triggered by underlying emotional issues, such as depression, anxiety, trauma, or low self-esteem. Addressing these underlying issues is a crucial part of recovery, as it can help individuals understand the root causes of their addiction and develop healthier coping mechanisms. This chapter will delve into the emotional landscape of gambling addiction and explore therapeutic approaches for healing the wounds that fuel the destructive cycle of gambling.

Unmasking the Emotional Triggers: Understanding the Why

Gambling addiction can serve as a way to escape from emotional pain, boredom, or feelings of emptiness. It can also be a way to self-medicate for underlying mental health conditions, such as depression or anxiety.

- **Depression:** The hopelessness and despair associated with depression can lead individuals to seek out the temporary excitement and distraction of gambling. The "high" of winning can provide a fleeting relief from the emotional pain of depression.

- **Anxiety:** Gambling can be a way to cope with anxiety, providing a temporary distraction from worries and fears. However, the financial stress and uncertainty of gambling can actually exacerbate anxiety in the long run.

- **Trauma:** Individuals who have experienced trauma may turn to gambling as a way to numb the pain of their past experiences. The adrenaline rush of gambling can provide a temporary escape from traumatic memories and emotions.

- **Low Self-Esteem:** Gambling can provide a false sense of control and accomplishment, boosting self-esteem in the short term. However, the losses and financial consequences of gambling can ultimately worsen feelings of inadequacy and worthlessness.

Therapeutic Approaches: Healing from Within

A variety of therapeutic approaches can be effective in addressing the underlying emotional issues that contribute to gambling addiction.

- **Individual Therapy:** Individual therapy provides a safe and confidential space for individuals to explore their emotions, identify triggers, and develop healthier coping mechanisms. Therapists can help individuals understand the root causes of their addiction and develop strategies for managing stress, anxiety, and other emotional challenges.

- **Group Therapy:** Group therapy offers a supportive environment where individuals can share their experiences, learn from others, and receive encouragement on their recovery journey. The shared experience of addiction can be incredibly validating and empowering.

- **Trauma-Focused Therapy:** For individuals who have experienced trauma, trauma-focused therapy can help them process their traumatic experiences and develop coping skills to manage triggers and flashbacks.

The Importance of Self-Compassion: A Key to Healing

One of the most important aspects of healing from gambling

addiction is developing self-compassion. Many individuals struggling with addiction are plagued by self-loathing and shame. They may believe they are weak, flawed, or undeserving of love and support.

Self-compassion involves recognizing that everyone makes mistakes, that addiction is a complex issue with many contributing factors, and that you are worthy of love and support, regardless of your past struggles. It involves treating yourself with kindness, understanding, and forgiveness.

Practicing self-compassion can help individuals break free from the cycle of shame and self-blame that often fuels addiction. It can also create a more positive self-image, increase self-esteem, and foster a sense of hope for the future.

Healing the emotional wounds of gambling addiction is a gradual process that requires patience, perseverance, and a commitment to self-care. By addressing the underlying emotional issues that contribute to addiction, individuals can break free from the destructive cycle of gambling and create a life filled with joy, peace, and emotional well-being.

RELAPSE PREVENTION STRATEGIES

Recovery from gambling addiction is a journey, not a destination. It's a continuous process of growth, healing, and self-discovery. While the initial steps of breaking free from addiction are crucial, the real challenge lies in maintaining long-term recovery and preventing relapse. This chapter will delve into the essential strategies for relapse prevention, equipping individuals with the tools and knowledge they need to stay on track and build a sustainable, fulfilling life beyond gambling.

Understanding Relapse: A Common Hurdle

Relapse is a common occurrence in recovery from addiction, and gambling addiction is no exception. It's important to understand that relapse is not a sign of failure or weakness. It's simply a setback, a temporary detour on the road to recovery. What matters is how you respond to the relapse and the steps you take to get back on track.

Triggers and Warning Signs: Recognizing the Red Flags

One of the most important aspects of relapse prevention is recognizing the triggers and warning signs that can lead to a slip. These can be internal, such as stress, boredom, or negative emotions, or external, such as social situations, financial difficulties, or exposure to gambling environments.

By identifying your triggers, you can develop strategies to avoid or cope with them. For example, if you know that stress triggers your urge to gamble, you can practice relaxation techniques, such as deep breathing or meditation, to manage your stress levels.

Creating a Relapse Prevention Plan: Your Roadmap to Success

A relapse prevention plan is a personalized roadmap that outlines the steps you will take to prevent relapse and maintain your recovery. It should include:

- **Identifying triggers:** As mentioned above, recognizing your triggers is the first step in avoiding them.
- **Developing coping skills:** Learn healthy ways to cope with stress, anxiety, boredom, and other emotions that may trigger gambling. This could include exercise, hobbies, spending time with loved ones, or seeking professional help.
- **Building a support network:** Surround yourself with supportive people who understand your struggles and encourage your recovery. This could include family, friends, therapists, or support groups.
- **Creating a healthy lifestyle:** Maintaining a healthy lifestyle can improve your overall well-being and reduce the risk of relapse. This includes eating a balanced diet, getting regular exercise, and getting enough sleep.
- **Avoiding risky situations:** Identify and avoid situations where you might be tempted to gamble. This could include avoiding casinos, online gambling sites, or social situations where gambling is prevalent.

Building a Life Beyond Gambling: Filling the Void

Gambling addiction often leaves a void in a person's life. Once gambling is removed, it's important to fill that void with healthy and fulfilling activities. This could involve:

- **Pursuing new hobbies and interests:** Discover new passions and activities that bring you joy and fulfillment. This could include sports, music, art, volunteering, or spending time in nature.
- **Building meaningful relationships:** Connect with loved ones and build strong, supportive relationships. This could involve spending quality time with family and friends, joining social groups, or volunteering in your community.
- **Setting goals:** Set achievable goals for yourself, both in your personal and professional life. This can give you a sense

of purpose and direction, and help you stay focused on your recovery.

The Power of Mindfulness: Staying Present

Mindfulness is the practice of paying attention to the present moment without judgment. It can be a powerful tool for managing cravings and preventing relapse. By focusing on the present moment, you can avoid getting caught up in thoughts of the past or worries about the future, which can trigger the urge to gamble.

Mindfulness practices, such as meditation, yoga, or deep breathing exercises, can help you cultivate a greater awareness of your thoughts and feelings, and develop the ability to respond to them in a healthy way.

A Lifelong Journey: Embracing the Challenge

Recovery from gambling addiction is a lifelong journey. It requires ongoing effort, self-reflection, and a commitment to growth. There will be challenges and setbacks along the way, but with the right strategies and support, you can overcome this addiction and build a fulfilling life beyond gambling.

Remember, relapse is not a failure, but an opportunity for growth. By learning from your mistakes and adjusting your relapse prevention plan, you can continue on your path to recovery and create a life filled with meaning, purpose, and joy.

STAYING ON TRACK: BUILDING A HEALTHY LIFESTYLE

Recovery from gambling addiction isn't just about abstaining from gambling; it's about rebuilding your life from the ground up. A crucial part of this process is cultivating a healthy lifestyle that supports your mental, emotional, and physical well-being. This chapter will explore the various aspects of a healthy lifestyle and how they can contribute to sustained recovery and overall happiness.

1. Nourishing Your Body: The Foundation of Well-being

The food you eat plays a significant role in your mental and emotional health. A balanced diet rich in fruits, vegetables, whole grains, and lean protein can provide the energy and nutrients your body needs to function optimally. Avoid processed foods, sugary drinks, and excessive caffeine, as these can negatively impact your mood and energy levels.

- Regular meals: Establish a routine of eating regular meals throughout the day to maintain stable blood sugar levels and avoid energy crashes that can trigger cravings.
- Hydration: Drink plenty of water throughout the day to stay hydrated and support cognitive function.
- Mindful eating: Pay attention to your hunger and fullness cues, and savor the flavors and textures of your food. This can help you avoid overeating and make healthier food choices.

2. Moving Your Body: Exercise for Mental and Physical Health

Regular exercise is not only essential for physical health but also plays a crucial role in mental well-being. Exercise releases endorphins, natural mood boosters that can help reduce stress, anxiety, and depression. It can also improve sleep quality, boost energy levels, and increase self-esteem.

- Find an activity you enjoy: Choose an exercise routine that you find enjoyable and sustainable. This could include walking, running, swimming, cycling, dancing, or any other activity that gets you moving.
- Aim for consistency: Strive for at least 30 minutes of moderate-intensity exercise most days of the week.
- Listen to your body: Pay attention to your body's signals and adjust your exercise routine as needed. Don't push yourself too hard, especially when you're starting.

3. Rest and Relaxation: Recharging Your Batteries

Adequate sleep is essential for both physical and mental health. When you're well-rested, you're better able to cope with stress, make sound decisions, and resist cravings. Aim for 7-8 hours of sleep per night, and establish a regular sleep schedule to promote restful sleep.

In addition to sleep, incorporating relaxation techniques into your daily routine can help reduce stress and promote overall well-being. This could include:

- Meditation: Meditation can help you focus on the present moment, calm your mind, and reduce anxiety.
- Deep breathing exercises: Deep breathing exercises can help you relax your body and reduce stress.
- Yoga: Yoga combines physical postures, breathing exercises, and meditation to promote relaxation and reduce stress.

4. Cultivating Healthy Relationships: The Power of Connection

Social connection is a fundamental human need. Strong, supportive relationships can provide a sense of belonging, purpose, and emotional support. In recovery from gambling addiction, healthy relationships can be a lifeline, offering encouragement, accountability, and a sense of community.

- Spend time with loved ones: Make time for meaningful interactions with family and friends. Engage in activities that you enjoy together, and be open and honest about your struggles and successes.
- Build new connections: Join social groups, clubs, or organizations that align with your interests. This can help you meet new people, expand your social circle, and build a support network.
- Seek out positive influences: Surround yourself with people who support your recovery and encourage healthy behaviors. Avoid negative influences that may trigger your urge to gamble.

5. Finding Meaning and Purpose: A Life Beyond Gambling

Recovery from gambling addiction involves more than just stopping the behavior; it's about creating a new life filled with meaning and purpose. This could involve:

- Pursuing your passions: Rediscover old hobbies or explore new interests. Engage in activities that bring you joy and fulfillment.
- Volunteering: Giving back to your community can provide a sense of purpose and connection. Volunteer your time and talents to a cause you care about.
- Setting goals: Set achievable goals for yourself, both in your personal and professional life. This can give you a sense of direction and motivation.
- Spiritual practices: Explore spirituality or religion if it resonates with you. This can provide a sense of meaning,

purpose, and connection to something larger than yourself.

Building a healthy lifestyle is an ongoing process, not a one-time event. It requires commitment, perseverance, and a willingness to make changes. By prioritizing your physical, mental, and emotional well-being, you can build a strong foundation for lasting recovery and a fulfilling life beyond gambling.

ONE DAY AT A TIME: LIVING IN THE PRESENT

In the tumultuous journey of recovery from gambling addiction, the concept of living "one day at a time" serves as a guiding principle, a lifeline for those navigating the treacherous waters of cravings, triggers, and the overwhelming weight of past mistakes. This chapter delves into the power of mindfulness and the importance of focusing on the present moment as a cornerstone of sustainable recovery.

The Tyranny of the Past: The Weight of Regret

Gambling addiction often leaves a trail of destruction in its wake. Financial ruin, broken relationships, lost opportunities, and a shattered sense of self can haunt individuals in recovery, making it difficult to move forward. The weight of regret and shame can be paralyzing, fueling a sense of hopelessness and despair.

However, dwelling on the past is counterproductive to recovery. It keeps you trapped in a cycle of guilt and self-blame, preventing you from focusing on the present and building a better future.

The Anxiety of the Future: The Fear of the Unknown

Just as the past can weigh heavily on the mind, the future can also be a source of anxiety and fear. Individuals in recovery may worry about relapsing, about never being able to fully overcome their addiction, or about the challenges that lie ahead. This fear of the unknown can be debilitating, preventing them from enjoying the present moment and taking steps towards a healthier future.

The Power of the Present Moment: Finding Peace and Clarity

The present moment is the only reality we have. It's where we experience life, where we make choices, and where we have the power to shape our future. By focusing on the present moment, we can break free from the tyranny of the past and the anxiety of the future.

Mindfulness, the practice of paying attention to the present moment without judgment, is a powerful tool for living in the present. It involves observing your thoughts and feelings without getting caught up in them, and focusing on the sensations of the present moment, such as your breath, your body, or the sounds around you.

Practicing mindfulness can help you:

- **Reduce stress and anxiety:** By focusing on the present moment, you can quiet your mind and reduce the stress and anxiety associated with the past and future.
- **Manage cravings:** Mindfulness can help you become more aware of your cravings and urges, allowing you to respond to them in a healthy way rather than giving in to them.
- **Improve self-awareness:** By paying attention to your thoughts and feelings, you can gain a deeper understanding of yourself and your triggers, which can help you make better choices and avoid relapse.
- **Cultivate gratitude:** Focusing on the positive aspects of your life and the things you are grateful for can help you develop a more optimistic outlook and reduce feelings of depression and despair.
- **Enhance enjoyment of life:** By being fully present in the moment, you can appreciate the simple joys of life and experience greater happiness and fulfillment.

One Day at a Time: A Philosophy for Recovery

The philosophy of "one day at a time" is a cornerstone of recovery from addiction. It emphasizes the importance of focusing on the present moment and taking things one step at a time.

By breaking down recovery into manageable chunks, individuals can avoid feeling overwhelmed and maintain their focus on the task at hand. Each day of sobriety is a victory, a testament to their strength and resilience.

Embracing the Journey: A New Perspective

Living in the present is not about ignoring the past or denying the future. It's about acknowledging the past, learning from it, and using those lessons to build a better future. It's about accepting the present moment as it is, with all its challenges and opportunities, and making the most of it.

By embracing the present moment, individuals in recovery can find peace, clarity, and the strength to continue on their journey to healing and wholeness.

FINDING NEW PASSIONS: REPLACING GAMBLING WITH PURPOSE

As the dust settles on the initial stages of recovery from gambling addiction, a void often emerges. The adrenaline rush, the thrill of the chase, and the social connections associated with gambling are no longer present. This void can be daunting, leaving individuals feeling lost, empty, and vulnerable to relapse. This chapter explores the importance of filling that void with new passions and pursuits, finding meaning and purpose in activities that promote well-being and personal growth.

The Danger of the Empty Void: A Breeding Ground for Relapse

The absence of gambling can create a vacuum in a person's life. The time and energy that were once devoted to gambling are now available, but without a clear direction, it can be tempting to fill that void with unhealthy habits or even return to gambling.

The emotional void left by gambling can be equally challenging. The excitement and stimulation associated with gambling can be replaced with feelings of boredom, restlessness, and dissatisfaction. These negative emotions can trigger cravings and increase the risk of relapse.

Rediscovering Your Passions: Igniting the Spark

One of the most effective ways to fill the void left by gambling is to rediscover old passions or explore new interests. Engaging in activities that bring you joy and fulfillment can provide a sense of purpose, boost self-esteem, and distract you from the urge to gamble.

- **Reconnect with old hobbies:** Think back to the things

you enjoyed doing before gambling took over your life. Did you love playing music, painting, writing, or participating in sports? Revisit these activities and see if they still spark your interest.

- **Explore new interests:** Try something new and exciting. Take a class, join a club, or volunteer for a cause you care about. Exploring new interests can open up new possibilities and help you discover hidden talents.

- **Set goals:** Setting achievable goals can give you a sense of purpose and direction. Whether it's learning a new skill, completing a project, or reaching a fitness milestone, working towards a goal can be incredibly motivating.

- **Challenge yourself:** Step outside of your comfort zone and try something that scares you a little. This could involve public speaking, learning a new language, or taking on a new challenge at work.

The Power of Purpose: A Life of Meaning

Finding new passions is not just about filling the void; it's about creating a life of meaning and purpose. Engaging in activities that align with your values and interests can give you a sense of fulfillment and satisfaction that gambling could never provide.

- **Helping others:** Volunteering your time and talents to help others can be incredibly rewarding. Whether it's mentoring a young person, assisting at a local shelter, or raising awareness for a cause you care about, giving back to your community can bring a sense of purpose and connection.

- **Pursuing your dreams:** Is there something you've always wanted to do but never had the time or courage to pursue? Now is your chance to chase your dreams and create a life that truly reflects your passions and values.

- **Leaving a legacy:** Think about the impact you want to have on the world. What do you want to be remembered for? By living a life of purpose, you can leave a lasting legacy that inspires others.

The Journey of Self-Discovery: A New Beginning

Replacing gambling with new passions is not just about finding activities to fill your time; it's about embarking on a journey of self-discovery. It's about exploring who you are beyond the addiction, discovering your true passions, and creating a life that is authentic and fulfilling.

This journey may not always be easy. There will be challenges and setbacks along the way. But with perseverance, self-compassion, and the support of loved ones, you can navigate this path and emerge stronger, happier, and more fulfilled than ever before.

SHARING YOUR STORY: HELPING OTHERS FIND THEIR WAY OUT

Recovery from gambling addiction is a deeply personal journey, but it's one that doesn't have to be taken alone. In fact, sharing your story can be a powerful tool for healing, not only for yourself but also for others who are struggling with similar challenges. This chapter explores the transformative power of sharing your experience, the benefits it offers to both the storyteller and the listener, and how you can use your story to inspire and empower others on their path to recovery.

The Power of Vulnerability: Breaking the Silence

Gambling addiction is often shrouded in secrecy and shame. Individuals may feel isolated and alone, afraid to speak out about their struggles for fear of judgment or rejection. However, breaking the silence and sharing your story can be a liberating experience.

- **Shattering the stigma:** By sharing your story, you help to challenge the stigma surrounding gambling addiction, showing others that they are not alone and that recovery is possible.
- **Inspiring hope:** Your story can be a beacon of hope for those who are still struggling, demonstrating that change is possible and that there is light at the end of the tunnel.
- **Building connection:** Sharing your experience can create a sense of connection and community, fostering a sense of belonging and support.

The Healing Power of Storytelling: Finding Meaning in Your Experience

Sharing your story can be a therapeutic process, helping you to make sense of your past experiences and find meaning in your struggles.

- **Processing emotions:** Storytelling allows you to express and process the complex emotions associated with addiction, such as shame, guilt, anger, and sadness.
- **Gaining perspective:** By reflecting on your journey, you can gain a new perspective on your experiences and learn valuable lessons that can help you move forward.
- **Building self-compassion:** Sharing your vulnerabilities can help you develop self-compassion, recognizing that you are not defined by your mistakes and that you are worthy of love and forgiveness.

Helping Others: Paying It Forward

Your story can be a powerful tool for helping others who are struggling with gambling addiction. By sharing your experience, you can:

- **Offer support and encouragement:** Your story can provide hope and inspiration to others, showing them that recovery is possible and that they are not alone.
- **Provide guidance and advice:** You can share the strategies and coping mechanisms that have helped you on your journey, offering practical advice to those who are just starting.
- **Raise awareness:** By speaking out about gambling addiction, you can help to raise awareness of this often-hidden problem and encourage others to seek help.

How to Share Your Story: Finding Your Voice

There are many ways to share your story, and the best approach will depend on your personal preferences and comfort level.

- **Talk to a therapist or counselor:** Sharing your story in a safe and confidential setting can be a powerful way to process your emotions and gain insights into your experiences.
- **Join a support group:** Support groups offer a safe space

to share your story with others who understand what you're going through.

- **Write about your experiences:** Writing can be a cathartic way to express your emotions and make sense of your past. Consider starting a journal, writing a blog, or even sharing your story in a book or article.

- **Speak out publicly:** If you're comfortable, you can share your story at public events, conferences, or online forums. This can help to raise awareness of gambling addiction and inspire others to seek help.

Sharing your story is a courageous act of self-love and service to others. It's a way to reclaim your power, find meaning in your experiences, and help others find their way out of the darkness of addiction. Remember, your story matters, and it has the power to change lives.

THE POWER OF CHOICE: TAKING BACK CONTROL OF YOUR LIFE

Gambling addiction can feel like a relentless force, stripping away your autonomy and leaving you at the mercy of impulses and cravings. However, at its core, recovery is about reclaiming the power of choice, rediscovering your agency, and forging a path towards a life defined by your own values and aspirations. This chapter delves into the transformative process of taking back control, exploring the psychological shifts, practical strategies, and empowering mindset that pave the way for lasting freedom from gambling addiction.

The Illusion of Helplessness: Breaking Free from the Victim Mentality

Gambling addiction often breeds a sense of helplessness, a belief that you are powerless to resist the urge to gamble. This victim mentality can be reinforced by the shame and guilt associated with addiction, leading to a feeling of being trapped in a never-ending cycle of despair.

However, this feeling of helplessness is an illusion. While addiction is a powerful force, it does not define you. You are not your addiction, and you have the power to choose a different path.

Reclaiming Your Power: The Choice to Change

The first step in taking back control is recognizing that you have a choice. You can choose to continue down the destructive path of addiction, or you can choose to seek help, make changes, and create a new life for yourself.

This choice may not be easy, especially in the early stages of recovery. Cravings and urges can be intense, and the temptation to gamble can be overwhelming. However, with the right support and strategies, you can learn to resist these urges and make healthier choices.

The Role of Self-Efficacy: Believing in Your Ability to Change

Self-efficacy, the belief in your ability to succeed, is a crucial factor in recovery. When you believe that you can change, you are more likely to take action, persevere through challenges, and achieve your goals.

Building self-efficacy involves setting small, achievable goals and celebrating your successes along the way. Each time you resist the urge to gamble or make a healthy choice, you reinforce your belief in your ability to change.

The Journey of Empowerment: A Life of Freedom and Choice

Taking back control of your life is a transformative process. It's about shedding the shackles of addiction and embracing your freedom to choose your own path. It's about discovering your own values, passions, and purpose, and living a life that is authentic and fulfilling.

The journey may not always be easy, but it is undoubtedly worth it. By reclaiming your power of choice, you can break free from the grip of gambling addiction and create a life that is truly your own.

A NEW NORMAL: CREATING A LIFE BEYOND GAMBLING

Recovery from gambling addiction is a transformative journey that involves not only breaking free from the destructive cycle of gambling but also creating a new, fulfilling life beyond it. This chapter delves into the process of building a "new normal," establishing a healthy and sustainable lifestyle that supports lasting recovery and fosters personal growth.

Embracing Change: The Path to a New Beginning

Recovery is a process of change, of letting go of old habits and embracing new ones. It's about redefining your identity, shifting your priorities, and creating a life that aligns with your values and aspirations.

This change can be both exciting and challenging. It requires stepping out of your comfort zone, facing your fears, and embracing the unknown. However, it also offers the opportunity for growth, self-discovery, and a renewed sense of purpose.

Building a Solid Foundation: Pillars of a Healthy Lifestyle

A new normal is built on a foundation of healthy habits and routines that support your physical, mental, and emotional well-being. These pillars include:

- **Healthy Eating:** Nourishing your body with wholesome, nutritious food provides the energy and nutrients you need to function optimally and reduces cravings.
- **Regular Exercise:** Engaging in regular physical activity releases endorphins, improves mood, reduces stress, and promotes overall health and well-being.
- **Quality Sleep:** Getting adequate sleep is essential for cognitive function, emotional regulation, and physical

health. Establishing a consistent sleep routine can help improve sleep quality and reduce fatigue.

- **Stress Management:** Developing healthy coping mechanisms for stress, such as mindfulness, meditation, or relaxation techniques, can help you manage triggers and avoid relapse.
- **Healthy Relationships:** Building strong, supportive relationships with family, friends, and therapists can provide a sense of belonging, encouragement, and accountability.

Rediscovering Joy: Finding Fulfillment in Everyday Life

A life beyond gambling is not about deprivation; it's about discovering new sources of joy and fulfillment. This could involve:

- **Pursuing Hobbies and Interests:** Rediscover old hobbies or explore new interests that bring you pleasure and satisfaction. This could include anything from painting and music to gardening and cooking.
- **Spending Time in Nature:** Connecting with nature has been shown to reduce stress, improve mood, and boost creativity. Take time to go for walks, hikes, or simply sit in a park and enjoy the beauty of the natural world.
- **Traveling and Exploring:** Discovering new places and cultures can broaden your horizons, ignite your curiosity, and create lasting memories.
- **Learning New Skills:** Challenging yourself to learn new skills, such as a new language, a musical instrument, or a sport, can boost confidence and provide a sense of accomplishment.
- **Giving Back:** Volunteering your time and talents to help others can be incredibly rewarding. It can give you a sense of purpose, connect you with your community, and make a positive impact on the world.

Navigating Challenges: Overcoming Obstacles

Building a new normal is not without its challenges. There will be setbacks, triggers, and moments of doubt. However, with the right tools and support, you can overcome these obstacles and continue on your path to recovery.

Embracing the Future: A Life of Freedom and Fulfillment

Creating a new normal is a process of transformation, of shedding the old and embracing the new. It's about building a life that is authentic, meaningful, and fulfilling. It's about discovering your passions, pursuing your dreams, and making choices that align with your values.

By embracing change, building a solid foundation, rediscovering joy, and navigating challenges with resilience and determination, you can create a new normal that is richer, more rewarding, and more fulfilling than you ever imagined.

HOPE FOR THE FUTURE:
THE PROMISE OF HEALING
AND GROWTH

The journey of recovery from gambling addiction is not just about overcoming a destructive habit; it's a transformative process that opens the door to healing, growth, and a renewed sense of purpose. This chapter delves into the profound potential for positive change that lies within the recovery process, exploring the emotional, psychological, and spiritual dimensions of healing and growth.

The Emergence of Resilience: Strength from Struggle

The experience of gambling addiction, while undoubtedly painful, can also be a crucible for growth. Overcoming addiction requires immense strength, courage, and resilience. It's a testament to the human spirit's ability to rise above adversity and find a path to healing.

As individuals navigate the challenges of recovery, they develop valuable coping skills, learn to manage their emotions, and build resilience in the face of adversity. They discover inner strength they never knew they had, and they emerge from the struggle stronger and more capable than before.

Rediscovering Your True Self: A Journey of Self-Discovery

Gambling addiction often masks a deeper struggle with identity and self-worth. Individuals may turn to gambling as a way to escape from emotional pain, to fill a void in their lives, or to cope with feelings of inadequacy.

Recovery provides an opportunity to shed the layers of addiction and rediscover your true self. It's a chance to explore your passions, values, and dreams, and to create a life that is authentic and meaningful. Through therapy, support groups, and self-reflection, individuals can gain a deeper understanding of themselves, their motivations, and their potential for growth.

Rebuilding Relationships: Stronger Connections

Gambling addiction can strain and damage relationships with family, friends, and loved ones. However, recovery offers the chance to rebuild those connections, often on a deeper and more meaningful level.

As individuals work to overcome their addiction, they learn to communicate more openly and honestly, to take responsibility for their actions, and to rebuild trust. They also develop a greater appreciation for the support and love of their loved ones, fostering stronger and more resilient relationships.

Finding Meaning and Purpose: A Life of Fulfillment

Recovery from gambling addiction is not just about stopping the destructive behavior; it's about creating a life filled with meaning and purpose. As individuals move beyond the grip of addiction, they often find new passions and pursuits that bring them joy and fulfillment.

This could involve volunteering their time to help others, pursuing creative endeavors, focusing on personal growth, or simply spending quality time with loved ones. By finding meaning and purpose in their lives, individuals in recovery can experience a profound sense of satisfaction and well-being.

Spiritual Growth: Connecting with Something Greater

For many individuals in recovery, spirituality or a connection to something greater than themselves plays an important role in their healing journey. This could involve exploring religious beliefs, practicing meditation or mindfulness, or simply connecting with nature and the world around them.

Spiritual growth can provide a sense of peace, hope, and purpose, helping individuals to find meaning in their struggles and to connect with a source of strength and wisdom beyond themselves.

Embracing the Future: A Life of Hope and Possibility

Recovery from gambling addiction is a journey of hope, healing, and growth. It's about more than just overcoming a destructive habit; it's about creating a new life filled with possibilities. By embracing change, seeking support, and focusing on the present moment, individuals can break free from the chains of addiction and embark on a path towards a brighter future.

The journey may be challenging, but the rewards are immeasurable. A life free from gambling addiction is a life filled with joy, peace, and the freedom to pursue your dreams.

BEYOND THE REEL: LIVING A LIFE OF FREEDOM AND FULFILLMENT

The journey of recovery from gambling addiction is a transformative odyssey, a passage from the depths of despair to the heights of self-discovery and fulfillment. This final chapter celebrates the triumph of the human spirit over adversity, illuminating the boundless possibilities that await those who have broken free from the chains of addiction.

A New Dawn: Embracing a Life of Freedom

Recovery is not merely an absence of gambling; it's a rebirth, a reawakening to the joys and possibilities of life. It's a chance to rewrite your story, to create a new narrative that is defined by your own values, passions, and aspirations.

As you step into this new chapter, you'll discover a newfound sense of freedom. The weight of addiction will lift, replaced by a lightness of being, a sense of liberation from the compulsive urges and destructive patterns that once controlled your life.

You'll rediscover the simple pleasures of life, the joy of spending time with loved ones, the satisfaction of pursuing your passions, and the peace of living in the present moment. You'll find that life beyond gambling is not only possible but also infinitely more fulfilling.

The Gift of Perspective: Learning from the Past

The experience of gambling addiction, while painful, can also be a source of profound wisdom and growth. It teaches you about your strengths and weaknesses, your triggers and vulnerabilities, and the importance of self-care and healthy boundaries.

By reflecting on your journey, you can gain valuable insights into the root causes of your addiction, the patterns that led you astray, and the strategies that helped you find your way back. These lessons can serve as a compass, guiding you towards a healthier and more sustainable path.

Building a Legacy: Paying It Forward

Your story of recovery is not just your own; it's a testament to the resilience of the human spirit and the power of hope. By sharing your experience, you can inspire and empower others who are struggling with addiction.

Whether it's through mentoring, volunteering, speaking at events, or simply sharing your story with friends and family, your journey can be a beacon of light for those who are still lost in the darkness of addiction. By paying it forward, you not only help others but also reinforce your own recovery and create a ripple effect of positive change.

Living a Life of Purpose: Making a Difference

Recovery from gambling addiction is an opportunity to redefine your purpose and make a meaningful contribution to the world. As you rediscover your passions and values, you may find yourself drawn to new career paths, volunteer opportunities, or creative endeavors that allow you to make a difference in the lives of others.

By using your experiences to help others, you can transform your pain into purpose, your struggles into strengths, and your setbacks into stepping stones towards a more fulfilling life.

Embracing the Journey: A Lifelong Commitment

Recovery is not a destination; it's a lifelong journey. It requires ongoing effort, self-reflection, and a commitment to personal growth. There will be challenges along the way, but with the tools and strategies you've learned, you can navigate these obstacles and continue to thrive.

Remember, recovery is not about perfection; it's about progress.

Celebrate your successes, learn from your setbacks, and never lose sight of the hope and possibility that lies ahead.

Beyond the Reel: Your Story Continues

Your story doesn't end with recovery; it's just the beginning. As you step into a life beyond the reel, you'll discover a world of possibilities, a life filled with joy, meaning, and purpose. You'll learn to embrace the present moment, cultivate healthy relationships, and pursue your passions with renewed vigor.

You'll find that recovery is not just about overcoming addiction; it's about discovering your true potential and living a life that is authentic, fulfilling, and inspiring. Your journey is a testament to the strength of the human spirit, and your story is a gift to the world.

www.ingramcontent.com/pod-product-compliance
Lightning Source LLC
Chambersburg PA
CBHW071953210526
45479CB00003B/917